T0363071

Daisy Jeffrey is a high school student and organiser in the school climate strikes, the most recent of which was one of the largest protests in Australian history, galvanising over 300,000 people to demand climate action. Daisy is also a fierce champion for gender equality. She lives in Sydney.

Writers in the *On Series*

Daisy Jeffrey

On Hope

hachette
AUSTRALIA

hachette
AUSTRALIA

Published in Australia and New Zealand in 2020
by Hachette Australia
(an imprint of Hachette Australia Pty Limited)
Level 17, 207 Kent Street, Sydney NSW 2000
www.hachette.com.au

10 9 8 7 6 5 4 3 2 1

A catalogue record for this
book is available from the
National Library of Australia

NATIONAL
LIBRARY
OF AUSTRALIA

ISBN: 978 0 7336 4466 5 (paperback)

Series cover design by Nada Backovic Design
Text design by Alice Graphics
Typeset by Kirby Jones
Printed and bound in Australia by McPherson's Printing Group

The paper this book is printed on is
certified against the Forest Stewardship
Council® Standards. McPherson's Printing
Group holds FSC® chain of custody
certification SA-COC-005379. FSC® promotes environmentally
responsible, socially beneficial and economically viable
management of the world's forests.

It's 6.30 am and there are already cameras in my face. As I storm through the house, anxiously throwing things into my backpack, I nervously laugh and answer questions on how I hope today's September 20 Global Climate Strike is going to go and what action we need our parliamentarians to take.

I haven't finished my speech.

I need to be in the Domain by 9.30 am for an interview with the *Australian Financial*

Review, so the film crew, Mum, and I roll out of the house and onto the next bus. As I walk towards the back, followed by an enormous camera, I hear a middle-aged bloke mutter to the passenger next to him, 'It's one of those bloody climate strikers.' Yeah, sorry, mate. It's me, one of those bloody kids trying to get our politicians to listen to the science – real inconvenience. Still, I feel a sudden urge to sit down and try to reason with him. My stomach tightens as I think about how many more people might share his point of view (if you're one of them and you're reading this little book, hopefully I can change your mind!) and then it contorts as my mind drifts towards the realisation that, yep, I've forgotten brekky.

We hop off the bus at Martin Place in the Sydney CBD and head up towards Macquarie Street. The sun is out but a cool breeze ruffles my hair. I'm supposed to look strong and determined for the camera, but in hindsight I think I might've beared more resemblance to a trembling weasel. I flinch as the breeze grows into a fierce wind – could this affect how the speeches carry across the crowd? Or worse, will it affect our numbers?

I reach the traffic lights and turn left onto Macquarie Street. My stomach is now twisting itself into knots and then, as we turn right into the Domain, it drops.

The Domain is an open grass plain in the Botanic Gardens, fenced in by enormous trees and the NSW Parliament House. In the far-left corner stands our excessively grand stage, adorned with an enormous banner that reads 'School Strike 4 Climate'. My fellow strike organisers – Varsha, Jean, India, Luca, Ambrose – and I, along with a dozen incredible volunteers painted it on Sunday when the strike was still six days in the future … Now, we only have two and a half hours to go. I still find myself panicking that no one will show up. Australia is spectacular at shouting about its lack of regard for authority and yet we have a remarkably unhealthy deference to it.

As our team is shuttled from camera to camera, we don't have time to figure out whether the journalists we're talking to have positive or negative intentions. The aim is to pump out the same message to the media as many times as possible in the hope that consistency will help it catch on. Essentially: the government's climate policy is beyond inadequate and it must change; and we have hope, but we need our state and federal governments to lead the change. Then there are our three demands:

1. No new coal, oil, or gas, including the Adani Carmichael coal mine.
2. One hundred per cent renewable energy generation and exports by 2030.
3. Fund a just transition and job creation for all fossil fuel workers and communities.

That third one gets the most questions, but I'll answer them later.

It's 11.30 am and I can still see enormous patches of green grass where placards and people should be. We've spent two and a half months organising this strike on top of schoolwork, at least three two-hour calls each week and who knows how many mental breakdowns … And for what? If no one shows up, we're back to square one.

But then the crowd starts pouring in, tens of thousands of kids brandishing colourful cardboard signs and bringing with them a palpable sense of optimism. Next come the uni students and I feel a sudden rush of affection for university politics that I'll never feel again. Then come the parents and the grandparents.

Looking fairly conspicuous in his yellow Knitting Nannas shirt (they're pretty cool, Google them), I spot Bill Ryan, a 97-year-old World War II veteran who has spent his life fighting against social injustice.

It's 11.50 am and I still haven't finished the speech – ah, bugger it, I'll wing it. I haul myself up on stage and, for the first time, I'm able to take in the enormity of the crowd. We did this. Not just our tiny band of organisers and everyone who helped put today together – but every single person who came out on the streets for climate justice. We are equally responsible for helping to fight for a better world.

I have a sudden flashback to a meeting we had with the cops in the lead-up to the strike where we assured the lovely nervous guy running the Domain that we could only possibly hit 40,000 strikers. As I look around me, I feel a little guilty because we have at least doubled that – oops.

'Pumped Up Kicks' (if you've been living under a rock, it's a jam from 2010) blasts through the speakers and Jean and I start dancing … in front of 80,000 people. We're terrible dancers, but we have an 80,000-strong crowd to help us. There is so much more to do today, but it doesn't seem so difficult anymore.

We can see swathes of passionate everyday Australians moving in unison, their voices blending in dissonant harmony. Waves of joy, anger and optimism crash over us as we belt out our demands. We scream, 'Each of these demands can be achieved. The only thing we lack is the political will!' We are exhausted, but our future depends on this and we can't afford to screw it up.

I have a composition assignment due at school today. Needless to say, I haven't handed it in. Briefly my mind drifts towards my looming HSC year and I suddenly feel indescribably angry. I'd like to be focusing on getting a good ATAR, but instead our parliament's gobsmacking inability to address climate change for what it is – a crisis – means that I and thousands of young people around Australia, have had to take on the challenge ourselves.

As I write this in December 2019, my friends are evacuating their homes while fires ravage towns and bush up and down the Australian east coast. They're scared because the fires have already claimed lives and ripped through over a million hectares of land, destroying native vegetation and wildlife. For some of them, the place they grew up in might not be there when they return. My city, Sydney, is suffocating under a thick blanket of yellow smoke and sometimes we wake up to a thin blanket of ash on the roofs of our cars.

How much more wildlife and how many more people will have to suffer before our state and federal governments finally take action?

*

In 2010, I was in Year 2 and sitting on the carpet of my friends' bedroom. We were saving the world. Niamh, Aoife and I had recently discovered the global waste crisis and, following clear selfless logic, we had concluded that eating chocolates and then collecting the foil wrappers was the best solution; a noble sacrifice. At home, I set up a Google blog, *The Environmentals*, on the chunky family PC. I also spent hours drafting a revolutionary design for a washing machine that relied on the circular rotation of magnets instead of electricity (for the record, I still think it's a cool idea).

I'd seen the then Shadow Minister for Communications, Malcolm Turnbull, on the news. I had no idea what his role was in politics (keep in mind, I was seven), but I knew he was one of the people meant to be helping run the country. I decided that he was the right person to share our idea with, so I wrote him a letter. I couldn't believe it took two seven-year-olds and an eight-year-old to solve the world's waste problem. The dream of becoming Young Australians of the Year dangled on the horizon.

Alas, it was not to be. A couple of weeks passed before I received a reply. Malcolm gently explained that there was a lot more to the problem than I was aware of and that, while he loved our enthusiasm, he couldn't use our idea. Although the dismissal hurt, my little wide eyes zoomed in on the encouragement. Seven-year-old me was stoked and ready to keep changing the world, although sadly chocolate-wrapper towers were now out of the question.

*

I grew up with the term 'global warming', which eventually morphed into 'climate change', a suspiciously less urgent term than its predecessor. Being a white middle-class city kid, I rarely witnessed the real-life impact this change was already having on rural, regional and Indigenous Australians. It wasn't until 2016, when I was in Year 8, that I saw a video of twelve-year-old Severn Suzuki, the daughter of Canadian environmental activist Dr David Suzuki, standing up at a global conference in 1992 and telling our leaders that something needed to be done about climate change. I couldn't believe how old the footage was. Writing this book, I realised that Severn could deliver the same speech today because it seems almost nothing has changed except for the amount of suffering our inaction is starting to inflict on communities around the globe.

I felt that sense of helplessness most of us experience when we know something desperately needs to change, but we don't feel like our voice could possibly make a difference. I felt it … for all of two weeks until an unrequited crush on a guy in my class swept it away from the forefront of my mind.

*

In February 2018, the world's heart broke when students at Marjory Stoneman Douglas High School in Parkland, Florida, were gunned down by a young white male. When the news cycle began to move on to the next tragedy, survivors decided that enough was enough and took to the streets. The March for Our Lives gun reform movement was born. It emerged out of necessity, a need to fight for a child's right to an education in a safe environment, and the culmination of decades of gun violence and mass shootings in American schools. On March 24, 2018, more than 1.2 million young people chose to use their voices to take to the streets and demand gun reform.

I'd never seen youth power like it. I don't think anyone had. We were all used to uni students heading out onto the streets to challenge injustice, but school students? Not so much. It was incredibly powerful and yet concerning because these kids should have been in school. They should have been singing rude songs in the playground, not chanting demands for gun reform. They should have been protected, not treated as an expendable consequence of the US second amendment. They should have been worrying about their exams, not about whether this was the day they'd get shot.

It is not unusual for young people to challenge the norm as they step out into the world, but they should not have to take to the streets to defend their classrooms from bullets. Similarly, we shouldn't have to defend our future from enormous fossil fuel corporations and greedy politicians. While the students in the U.S.A were marching for gun reform, the Australian government was pushing forward with approvals for the Adani Carmichael coal mine, a highly controversial project run by the equally controversial Indian multinational conglomerate Adani, a company fined more than once for breaching environmental laws and standards. It seemed our future was being consciously thrown away by our own politicians for short-term political gain. But what could I do about it?

The March for Our Lives movement led to a question forming at the back of my mind: would young people come together like this to demand climate action?

*

Many Australians have a potent sense of pride about not caring about politics, or at least in being indifferent to changes in leadership. Those of us who are enthralled by the political bubble will quite literally spend hours discussing election results and various politicians before someone else will point out that they have no idea who or what we're talking about.

On the night of the federal election, May 18, my grandparents were in a remote outback town, in a pub that, as my grandmother would assert with disbelief, didn't have wineglasses! One TV screen was showing rugby league and on the other you could watch Aussie Rules. Desperate to keep up with the election results, my grandparents and their circle of friends turned to their phones. As the night wound up, they commented on the Liberal election win to the bartender who responded, 'Oh did they? Doesn't make any difference to me.'

There's a middle ground between having a sad fascination with parliamentary politics, and having no interest at all. That middle ground makes for an informed voter and in a world where Clive Palmer can spend $60 million on a scare campaign that included inaccurate or misleading information without facing any repercussions, we need to step up and become informed.

So, how do we stay informed? Print media used to be the answer, but there are a couple of problems with that argument now, namely that most of us don't turn to print media for the news, and, if we do, some papers have political affiliations and don't always publish the news objectively. One spectacular example of this was during the 2019–2020 bushfire crisis, when the government had monumentally buggered up. On a day when the government's failure should have been headline news, *The Australian*'s front page was plastered with criticism of the ABC, student activists and the Labor Party, and an ominous warning of an imminent Islamic terror threat. Far be it from me to accuse the Murdoch media of deliberately misleading its readership, but that front page was a shocker and reflects blatant bias towards one side of politics.

Many of us now turn to social media to stay updated with the world, but social media is probably one of the worst places to get your news. Not only is the information you're reading likely to be inaccurate, but social media uses algorithms to show you news you're likely to agree with; news that confirms your own prejudices. This in turn encourages you to agree with a certain bunch of people with a similar political viewpoint, which further isolates you from content or people that may challenge your assumptions. I tend to 'like' more progressive content when I'm scrolling through Facebook and, over time, I've been directed to more progressive or leftist pages that encourage a certain point of view. It's almost impossible for me to see opinions other than my own unless I actively seek them out. So, I basically end up agreeing with myself without having to challenge my perceptions. Over the last decade, we've seen this process contribute to the polarisation of politics – this sense of belonging to a tribe. More and more, when we're approached by someone with a differing opinion to our own, we feel more inclined, and perhaps self-righteous enough, to shut it down.

For both sides of politics, this is a dangerous problem. The more we isolate ourselves, the more polarised our world becomes.

It wasn't until I joined the ABC's *Q&A* audience right after September 20 that I was really confronted with a different world perspective to my own. I was sitting next to a man who looked to be in his sixties and I immediately felt I knew which side of politics he was on. I introduced myself and he mentioned his affection for a Liberal MP on the panel. When I asserted that I did not share his affection, he glanced at my larger than life Stop Adani earrings and smiled in the way one smiles at a toddler who's just dribbled food down their front. After a pause he said, 'I like to rely on the facts, your side of politics relies on emotion.' My brain went into meltdown. What on earth? What thought process did he go through to come to that conclusion? Instead of self-combusting, I chose to probe further. 'What do you mean, my side relies on emotion?' He went on to explain that the left is too emotional and alarmist, they'd never be able to lead the country, whereas the current government could.

I was shocked to be confronted with an outlook so starkly in contrast with my own, especially after spending months comfortably isolated in my own tribe, but it was also invigorating. I wanted to talk to him for hours, but I had to settle for five minutes. I began shooting off a round of questions. Where did he find his news? Conservative media. What facts was he referring to? Would he be open to changing his opinion? Yes, of course, but he felt he knew how the world worked and that a young person such as myself would eventually grow up and understand.

I was ecstatic. As I began to reason with him, he conceded that we should act according to the science, but what about the economy? I responded by saying that we needed to act thirty years ago when the science first emerged and that while a transition to renewable energy would be expensive now, an emergency switch down the track would cost far more. His concern was the loss of jobs if mines like the Adani Carmichael project were closed down.

I countered with the fact that the Adani mine would soon be almost entirely automated so the thousands of jobs the government and Adani had promised were little more than fiction. Also, the Adani Carmichael mine threatens the 60,000 current jobs that rely on the Great Barrier Reef tourism industry. He then accused my 'lot' of wanting to switch to renewable energy overnight. I tried again to say that a just transition to renewable energy and job creation for fossil fuel workers and their communities were equally important and urgent issues.

Our 'debate' was brought to an end by the *Q&A* theme music. We certainly hadn't come to an agreement, but at least we had reached an understanding of each other's point of view.

*

As we venture further into a world where our lives are dominated by social media, it's crucial that we search for answers outside of our comfort zone. We must make the effort not to cherrypick our evidence. We must search for the facts.

We cannot trust one news source to provide us with all the answers. We need to make the effort to listen and read widely. I read *The Daily Telegraph* and *The Australian*, as well as the ABC, *The Guardian* and *The New York Times*. You definitely don't need to read this widely, but it's vital to hear both sides of the story to determine what's valid and what might've been warped to suit someone's agenda.

At a certain point, however, we should stop encouraging the media to report both sides of a debate as if they're equal, particularly the climate change versus climate denial debate. When 97 per cent of the scientific consensus states climate change is manmade, it becomes clear which side is valid. Put it this way: if you were on your way to board a plane and as you crossed the tarmac you passed one hundred mechanics – would you trust the ninety-seven who said the engines were faulty and urgently needed maintenance? Or would you trust the three who told you there was nothing to worry about?

This is the climate 'debate': 97 per cent of the world's leading climate scientists have identified that humankind has contributed heavily to climate change, but somehow the three per cent who dissent are heard just as loudly in the media, presenting a fake two-sided debate.

*

I first heard about the school strikes for climate action on November 23, 2018, through the mums running the canteen at my school, the Conservatorium High School in Sydney. They knew Jean Hinchliffe, the fourteen-year-old girl running the strikes, and thought I would want to get involved. I rushed home that afternoon and looked up the Facebook event – November 30, 12 pm, NSW Parliament House on Macquarie Street. Easy, it was a ten-minute stroll up the road from my school. I printed out a bunch of permission templates off the new School Strike website and created a sign-up sheet. I then went onto our school's student Facebook group and typed out a message about the strike and why I thought it would be worth missing class for. The next day, I made an announcement at the school assembly – something I would not be able to do for the September 20 Strike, but I digress.

I had many conversations with students that week in 2018 who wanted to go, but who wouldn't miss class without a good reason. Then on November 26, Prime Minister Scott Morrison announced that 'there should be less activism and more learning in schools' and the media went ballistic. I love that, against Scott's wishes, his statement probably contributed to the enormous student turnout more than anything else. Our whole school was abuzz talking about the climate strike. Many of us knew we needed more climate action, but none of us knew just how many young people would take to the streets to get it.

On November 30 at 11.30 am, more than thirty Con High students walked out of class, carefully designed signs in hand, and began walking up towards Martin Place (the numbers were now too big for NSW Parliament House). We reached a silent Parliament House and my heart sank – what if no one showed up? What if we turned the corner and we were the handful of students who cared enough to risk retribution for demanding our government listen to the science?

And then we saw it.

A sea of uniforms and cardboard placards, sweltering in the November heat. Cheers rang out through the crowd and adults pressed their faces up against the windows of surrounding twenty-storey buildings to catch a glimpse of this phenomenon. We wove our way through the crowd to try to find a good viewing spot. We couldn't hear a word of the speeches – even the audio-visual system wasn't prepared for this many people – but we joined in as the whooping travelled back through the crowd. It felt like the beginning of something huge, but I don't think any of us could have imagined what this fledgling movement would grow to be in less than a year.

On the bus home, I wrote out a long message about how much I wanted to get involved and sent it through to the School Strike Facebook page. An excruciatingly long five minutes later, I was added to the Sydney organising chat. I didn't know it then, but this was the beginning of a journey that would change my life in ways I could never imagine. That first night, I jumped on a call and was stunned when I was confronted with a bunch of schoolkids just like me. We were exhausted, with dark circles under our eyes, but wildly optimistic about our ability to make a difference to the world. With a 15,000-student turnout nationwide under our belt, we had announced another protest – March for Our Future on December 8, now only one week away. I was asked if I'd like to speak and I eagerly put my hand up for the job.

The night before the march, I was staying at a friend's and everything that could possibly go wrong went wrong – my phone drowned in a puddle of water and my laptop decided to stop turning on. I was going to have to do this the old-fashioned way: I was going to have to write my speech out by hand. Yeah, I can hear you over-twenties laughing at my tech dependence. Not only this, but I had the fattest crush on one of the guys at the sleepover, so I didn't end up writing the speech until I was on a bus, hurtling towards the city the next morning.

As we neared the CBD, I kept running sentences and syntax by my friends, neither of whom was wildly enthusiastic to listen to my frantic last-minute speech writing. I wanted to fact-check things, but my phone screen was now a wondrous rainbow of fluorescent greens, yellows and pinks.

When I eventually stood up at the microphone that day, I was so nervous that my voice shook, but my nerves were met with cheers.

Sociologist and activist Eva Cox says there is a certain orgasmic feeling that accompanies going out and protesting something. You feel like you're really making a difference, but then you usually go home and carry on with your normal life, leaving the will to fight for change at the front door.

Many adults have told us that we give them hope. You may have even told someone that yourself, but we're not kidding when we say we don't want your hope. Yes, we appreciate it, but we'd much rather be at school and not having to pile activism on top of our academic education. As former Greens leader Bob Brown excellently put it when I called to interview him about the Stop Adani campaign, hope is a useless little four-letter word ... unless it's accompanied by action.

Put simply, the best way to thank an activist is to join them.

*

In 2019, Bob Brown headed a convoy of activists who travelled up the east coast and into regional Queensland to protest the proposed Adani Carmichael coal mine. The convoy was heavily criticised by both major parties and the media. It was also blamed for having a hand in the Coalition's election win. Naturally, curiosity got the better of me and I called Bob to ask him a few questions.

Everyone I know had asked the same question, 'What were they thinking?' Southerners going up into the Sunshine state to protest against the livelihoods of regional Queenslanders – how did they think that was going to go? Well, according to Bob, it went exactly as expected. He brought me back to the Franklin River campaign, a late seventies fight by the Wilderness Society to keep the Tasmanian Franklin River from being turned into a dam.

Just like Stop Adani, the Franklin River campaign was accused of trying to take away people's jobs. And just like today, these accusations were perpetuated by the corporations and the government who stood to profit from the dam. After the Franklin River campaign was won by environmentalists, the facts propagated by the hydroelectric commission surrounding the dam's job creation capacity were found to be false.

Bob told me that the media failed to report how the Stop Adani convoy was received by the Wangan and Jagalingou people in Clermont whose native title had been extinguished by the Queensland government to make way for the Adani mine. This meant that native titleholder's objections to the mine no longer held the same legal significance and that they could now be forcibly removed from their traditional lands by police.

When I asked Bob to tell me what he'd seen up in regional Queensland, he said it was impossible to be in Townsville and miss Adani. The company had dug roots into the Queensland community by funding local groups and events. He also commented on the corporation's supposed ability to create 10,000 jobs. This job creation scheme, he pointed out, failed to account for the jobs in the Great Barrier Reef tourism industry that would be drastically affected by Adani's decision to export coal out over the reef.

According to the Australian Marine Conservation Society:

> If Adani's mine goes ahead it will be
> one of the largest coal mines in the

world and will generate an estimated 4.7 billion tonnes of carbon pollution over its lifetime. At a time when we need to be reducing our carbon pollution to save our reef – this is reckless beyond belief ... Adani exceeded its permitted pollution discharge limit to the Great Barrier Reef World Heritage Area by more than 800 per cent at the Port of Abbot Point, and spilt coal-laden water into the neighbouring fragile Caley Valley Wetlands, and onto the beach next to the Great Barrier Reef World Heritage Area.

We know Australia has a responsibility to move to renewable energy. While domestically, our emissions may not amount to much, our coal exports place us as the third largest emissions exporter behind Russia and Saudi Arabia. Not only this, but taxpayers are spending billions of dollars each year subsidising the fossil fuel industry.

My grandad left the UK in the seventies to come out and work in Australian mines. He was a coal-mining engineer, something he was deeply proud of throughout his life. He brought with him his Hungarian wife, my dad and his sister, and his two step-kids.

When the industry tightened in the eighties, Grandad was made redundant. His decades of work and experience suddenly meant nothing. Following a rather dramatic divorce (let's not go into that), he was now a single father with two kids, with no means of providing. Presented with no alternative, he became a cleaner. When he became sick with pneumonia, the local church community took care of my dad and his younger sister.

In his later years, in the grips of dementia, Grandad used to sit me down on our red sofa and tell me stories over and over about his time down in the mines. He was so proud of having worked around the world to make coal mines safer.

When we talk about a just transition, we're talking about ensuring job creation for everyone affected by the transition to renewable energy. One of the first things I noticed coming into the climate movement was the ambiguity surrounding a just transition, both from politicians and activists. Many would say those two words over and over again, but when queried on the subject, could not substantiate their argument. As a result, most people working in the fossil fuel industry have little trust in those two words anymore because their purpose is rarely anything other than a political ploy.

Although conditions and pay have improved immensely due to the tireless work of unions since my grandad's redundancy, coal mining is still many families' way of putting food on the table; as well as their identity and their community's means of survival.

Both major parties frequently talk about towns whose economies are reliant on the fossil fuel industry and both acknowledge that we need to move to renewable energy. Yet, neither the Liberal Party nor Labor brought a convincing and thought-through transition policy to the last federal election. We need to move to renewable energy, but how can we expect those whose lives depend on the fossil fuel industry to support a transition when no one is showing a practical pathway that will support them and their community.

When I walk into a meeting, I'm often the youngest person in the room and although I have an enormous amount of privilege as a white cisgender person, I've noticed that my age and gender drastically affect how people interact with me. Sometimes I'm completely ignored or someone will repeat a point I just made and proceed to take credit for it. Activists and politicians are keen to meet with us and take a photo, but usually have little intention of actually listening to what we have to say. All of us in the school strike movement have had to figure out different ways of framing our messaging so our voices are heard.

I particularly noticed this disparity in the power imbalance of older versus younger voices when I tried to get information from various politicians and activist groups about a just transition. When I asked the NSW unions about the whereabouts of this mythical transition policy, I was told many different stories, each as confusing as the next. What became clearer and clearer was that there was a fantastic amount of miscommunication between the climate movement and the mining unions and that to move forward we would need to build a bridge over this hostility.

We are now seeing regional communities and economies being devastated by floods, drought and fire as Australia continues to let its emissions rise. On both sides of politics, there is finally a sense of inevitability surrounding a transition to renewable energy, but the reality is we're not moving fast enough. Whether we like it or not, Australia has a significant part to play in taking climate action and this action requires urgent bipartisan support for the funding of a just transition program for all fossil fuel workers and communities. We need unions to lead the way.

*

Much of Australia seems to be suffering from a 'my voice won't make a difference' epidemic. Call me naïve, but I've always been psyched to get out and vote, a mindset I found out three weeks before the federal election, wasn't shared by most Aussies. Day after day I'd hear stories from friends and acquaintances about how they felt their voice wasn't being heard and therefore didn't matter. Then I discovered some people would enter the ballot booth, tick randomly and then stick their vote in the ballot box as a 'throwaway vote'. It was surreal to hear so many people all say the same thing, 'My voice doesn't matter.'

I wanted to sit the thousands, possibly millions of voters with this outlook down together and ask them to repeat what they'd told me because maybe then they'd see that one voice is more than enough to make a difference. Yes, one vote can be little more than a drop in the ocean, but when those millions of discarded votes are used to represent genuine concerns, they become a tidal wave of change.

I did at least put these sentiments in my speech for the first Global Climate Strike on March 15, 2019. We'd upped our previous strike numbers tenfold – 150,000 people across Australia and 1.6 million across the globe. Surely, we couldn't get any bigger than this? (Spoiler: we did!)

Standing in front of the crowd, arguing for the importance of voting for climate action, I realised that 90 per cent of the strikers were, like me, too young to vote. If we couldn't vote, would either major party see enough of a risk to their primary vote to promise ambitious climate action, or even adequate action? My heart sank a little as I contemplated another Liberal–National Coalition government; not that Labor would've been much better, but at least they *had* a functioning climate policy.

So, why did we vote against climate action?

On May 18, 2019, the federal election was won and Scott Morrison finished his almost presidential campaign with a victorious, 'We're going to keep the promise of Australia for all Australians', whatever that means. No, seriously, if you've cracked the code, please chuck me an email. Anyway, Morrison was sworn in as prime minister and many commentators took this as an indication that

Australians simply didn't care enough about the climate to vote for a party that had a legitimate climate policy. While there are a number of factors that contributed to the Liberal–Nationals win – Clive Palmer's $60 million campaign being one of them – the commentators' view might be true because it is so easy to dismiss an issue when it isn't directly affecting you. If you are, in this moment, completely safe from the effects of climate change, it's all too easy to push it from your mind. When voting, the decision usually comes down to what we perceive as affecting our immediate wellbeing and, until the recent bushfire crisis, many Australians were not experiencing the real-life ramifications of climate change.

As a consequence, electoral politics is geared towards responding to immediate grievances. What it isn't so good at is mitigating an underlying problem. It's like being faced with a gaping wound and reaching for the band-aids. Our parliamentarians need to be creating and funding long-term solutions, such as acting in accordance with the climate science and creating policy that will help Australia minimise the potential ramifications of climate change. Instead, the government has put out a $2 billion bushfire relief package and announced that they have no intention of creating a more robust climate policy.

What the government wasn't banking on was the sheer amount of anger from bushfire survivors, firefighters and volunteers, and the general public. While we mightn't have voted in favour of climate action, we were now making our voices heard. There have been a number of bushfire-related protests that have popped up on Facebook with a week's notice, maybe less, and have drawn tens of thousands of Australians out onto the streets. While these protests may be ill-equipped to achieve specific demands, they do showcase the shifting tectonic plates in public opinion. Climate is moving to the top of the agenda and, as Australia continues to bear the pain of increasingly worsening fires, flooding and drought, we seem to have little intention of letting it fall off the agenda again.

Rewind to election night on May 18, 2019, the fifty weary teenagers who jumped on a midnight call to discuss what we would do next could never have expected the community response to these fires. Our hope had been dwindling, but the election results sparked a new sense of determination to get the action Australia so desperately needed (and still needs). We settled on September 20 for the second ever Global Climate Strike.

*

It's 8.30 am in August 2019 and I'm struggling to process the maths being written out on the smart board. The bright, almost clinical lights beat down on me as I scrawl theory across my notebook. Just four and a half hours earlier I was discussing strategy on an international call with strikers from around the globe. The reality of having been awake and engaged at four in the morning three times in one week has caught up with my brain, which is now screaming for sleep. My eyelids desperately droop and my torso leans towards the table and … I'm conked.

Thirty minutes later I wake up and heave myself off to my next class. I remind myself that this isn't sustainable – this is the tail end of Year 11 after all – but then I remember that we have a month and a half until September 20, so I reassure myself that a strong flat white will fix everything. What could go wrong?

How do I balance activism and school? School strikers get asked this question all the time, both by students and adults. I'd love to say that I'm completely on top of things, that I'm that freakishly organised person who can take everything life throws at them but, as you might be able to tell by now, I'm not. It's all a bit of a shemozzle really. My mind is always in a million different places at once – trig over here, Adani over there and a desperate need for coffee at the front. I should not have to be doing this. This is the government's responsibility, not mine. My generation's only current concern should be our next identity crisis and exam week, but instead the worsening impacts of climate change are clouding our future.

Despite what I've just written, we're not as pessimistic as you might think. We get wrapped up in our own little dramas. I find hope in the laughter I hear at school and happiness in the tall sunflowers around the corner from my house. I find hope in the eyes and voices of the young people who strike for climate action. I hear it in the excited voices of adults congratulating young people on our activism, although sometimes an adult placing their hope upon us can feel more like a burden than encouragement.

When I was initially asked to write this book, it was titled 'On Change' which, if you ask me, is a hell of a lot easier than 'On Hope'. Writing about hope requires hopefulness, which I find is sometimes in short supply, particularly when the world really does feel like it's falling apart.

That month before the strike left no room for despair, however. I was in a constant state of caffeine-fuelled panic, running from a meeting with union officials to a meeting with tech corporation Atlassian's co-founder and resident billionaire climate activist Mike Cannon-Brookes. From there, I'd rush back home to work on assignments and jump into a meeting with the NGOs helping us with logistics on strike day. You'd think it'd end there, but no. At 7.30 pm, I'd be chastised for not being available for dinner with the fam, but I'd grab my meal and head up to my room for a national coordination call with strikers across Australia. We were all exhausted, but there was an undeniable aura of excitement. Superannuation fund Future Super had recently created a petition for businesses to support the school strikes, titled 'This is Not Business as Usual'. It was gaining media traction and, though we didn't know it at the time, it would grow to well over three thousand businesses by the day of the strike.

Back at school, the NSW Department of Education was putting more pressure than ever on principals and teachers to prevent their students from attending the strikes. I'd been able to announce the previous two climate strikes at the school assembly without any issues, so long as I wasn't going to go on a passionate spiel about our state and federal governments' inaction. This time was different. Midway through my announcement that everyone should probably get their parents to sign a note permitting them to attend, my principal stormed across the stage to declare that the school 'does not have a stance on politics'. It seemed unnecessary and almost frantic. I was startled by the sudden outburst and just stood still, dumbfounded. The whole school tittered and the assembly was immediately over. As I walked out of the hall, one of my teachers (who is no longer at the school) compared the pressure from the Department of Education to communist Hungary. I began to laugh and then something incredible happened … Students began approaching me to renew their commitment to attend the strike. Just like Scott Morrison's outburst prior to the first strike, the department's pressure had backfired.

On September 16, in the midst of the raging NSW abortion debate and with just four days until the strike, six drenched students trudged into NSW Parliament House to hear a motion read out in the senate in favour of the school strikes. Dani, Jean, Varsha, Luca, Ambrose and I sat in the tiny public gallery, hemmed in by anti-choice protesters. During one senior senator's impassioned speech against the legalisation of abortion, I let out a small exasperated chuckle, which caused the greatest offence to a woman two rows in front of me. She turned around and aggressively stared at me for the duration of the speech, which made the whole experience even more hilarious.

Much to our surprise, we found out the NSW Minister for Energy and Environment, Matt Kean, was keen to meet with us, but it would have to wait a couple of hours. A Labor senator kindly offered us her office until the meeting, so we crammed in and started on our homework. We were like family by this point.

Months of dedication to this existential crisis had become the glue that bonded a small bunch of unlikely friends together. Varsha Yajman would go on to achieve a 99.15 ATAR, so clearly activism wasn't impacting her schoolwork.

We weren't sure what to expect with Matt Kean. Our experience with politicians told us that he'd likely talk at us for five minutes and then want to take a photo, but we found a quite different story when we sat down with him. He pushed back meetings to listen and talk with us for forty minutes and, while I strongly disagree with his staunch belief in capitalism, I gained a huge amount of respect for him.

It's important to be a little cynical when a politician tells you anything, but Matt insisted that he was pushing for more ambitious climate action and I desperately wanted to believe him. He was apparently the first Liberal NSW Minister for Energy and Environment that activist groups had been able to negotiate with in years. I have hope that he will follow through, particularly in light of how consistently outspoken he's been in terms of pushing for more climate action. (On January 20, 2020, some of his comments provoked public criticism from Scott Morrison who complained that Matt didn't know what he was talking about and that the federal cabinet probably didn't even know who he was.)

Later that night, our small team, once more soaked in the rain, would travel to the Amnesty International offices to receive the

Ambassador of Conscience Award 2019 in recognition of our climate activism.

The night before the second Global Climate Strike on September 20, 2019, the Sydney team came to stay at my house. We set up a corkboard in the corner of my living room with a timetable for the next morning tightly pinned to it. All of us had interviews at around six or seven, so we'd have to pack up and move out fast. We laughed until sometime past one in the morning whereupon we realised we'd be royally screwed if we didn't get some sleep.

And that brings us back to the beginning, but I'll give you a quick run-through, just in case you've forgotten.

There was a lot of panic, then the realisation that we'd hit 80,000 people, then a lot of joy, then the realisation we'd hit 330,000 people nationwide, then 6 million worldwide. Dani, Varsha and I jumped on the train to head to the ABC for another interview and everything seemed oddly quiet. We'd just done the impossible. What would we do next?

That night I arrived home, donned some corduroy pants and a crop, and then headed off to my Year 11 social, which was infinitely less exciting than trying to save the world.

*

After September 20, it felt like my profile exploded. Media outlets were reaching out to me left and right to get a comment on government inaction and even News Corp's Chris Kenny wrote a conspiracy theory piece on how I was being controlled by the Labor Party – kudos on having a wild enough imagination to draw that conclusion. However, I realise and choose to note here that two major factors in my growing platform were and are my being inner-city and white. The media loves to whitewash the climate movement, a prime example being an incident in January 2019 where a media outlet cropped my friend, Ugandan climate striker Vanessa Kate, from a photo with Greta Thunberg and three other Caucasian strikers.

White women are not the only people fighting for climate justice, so why does the media portray it that way? In Canada, there is Autumn Peltier, an Indigenous fourteen-year-old girl fighting for the protection of the Great Lakes.

In Scotland, you will find trans climate activist Dylan Hamilton. In the United States, Xiye Bastida, a member of the Indigenous Mexican Otomi-Toltec nation, is fighting for climate justice. Here in Australia, Amelia Telford, an Aboriginal and South Sea Islander woman from Bundjalung country is the National Director of the Seed Indigenous Youth Climate Network.

Here in Australia and across the globe, those on the frontlines of climate change are being ignored. Indigenous, rural and regional voices are all but wiped from the media in favour of voices like Greta Thunberg's and mine. This is not to discredit Greta. She has been a catalyst in reorienting the conversation around climate, however, there are so many important stories still waiting to be heard.

In October, internationally renowned popstar Shawn Mendes's team reached out to set up a lunch with School Strike 4 Climate. As I headed towards his hotel on November 2, I had absolutely no idea as to what to expect. I hadn't listened to his music, but I had seen the online frenzy surrounding his relationship to fellow popstar Camila Cabello. However, when my friend Jean and I sat down with Shawn and his manager, Cez, to discuss all things climate, reality painted a very different picture to the one featured in the celebrity media.

He exuded a fantastically Canadian politeness and frequently spoke about his younger sister. As we dug into our ridiculously fancy meals (which were excellent by the way – I intensely resented having to go back to normal person food), I realised he was just another young person, albeit an incredibly successful musician, looking for a way to use his voice effectively. That night, our small team was invited to attend his concert. We sat almost at the very front, hemmed in by thousands of screaming fans. However, nothing could have prepared us for the sheer cacophony of enthusiasm that accompanied Shawn's entrance.

There was so much joy up on that stage and it reverberated around the arena. For two hours, we were wrapped up in one person's passion and the outside world seemed to fall away. As I looked around, even the disgruntled partners of committed fans found themselves swaying to the music. At the end of the night, photos and videos were taken, and a ticket was signed for my little brother who absolutely lost it when I returned home to present it.

A few months later, Shawn would post a photo of his guitar with 'CLIMATE ACTION NOW' taped on the back – a small gesture, some have pointed out, but I think it was a pretty big step away from the centre for him. In addition to this, his foundation also made a donation to the school strike movement here in Australia. We need those with similar platforms to consistently be advocating for climate justice.

*

In December 2019 – three months after the Global Climate Strike – I was invited to attend the UN Climate Conference in Madrid (also known as COP25) … What a rollercoaster of an experience that was.

As I boarded the flight, I had two things on my mind:

1. Would this conference achieve anything?
2. Bugger, I'd better start on that English assignment.

So, I did. I filled the first nine hours with maths and English. For the first time in forever, I delved into schoolwork and left activism at the door. It was a relief because it felt like a massive weight had been lifted off my shoulders. Then I landed in Hong Kong, connected to the wi-fi and my messages came flooding through – back to reality.

I was staying in a hostel in Madrid with six others – strikers from Uganda, Russia and Chile who I'd get to know and love over the coming week. Ugandan striker Vanessa was nearly at her sixtieth consecutive day of striking to protect the Congo Rainforest and explained that it was almost impossible to strike in numbers due to the political climate in her country. Russian striker Sasha was facing a similar problem. One of her co-organisers, Arshak, was facing a trial and a possible jail sentence when they got back to Russia. His crime? Organising a three-person climate strike without a permit. Sasha explained that Arshak had repeatedly contacted authorities about a permit but hadn't received a response.

On Monday, we heaved ourselves out of bed at 6.30 am, chowed down some brekky, and headed out into the crisp winter air. The metro was full of people with the same destination as us – 30,000 human beings all hoping to make the world a better place. As we arrived, the enormous blue COP25 sign came into view. I was in awe – I was about to enter the place where countries from all over the world come together to make change. We checked our bags and badges through security and headed inside.

Imagine ten Bunnings Warehouses strung together and you have the COP25, only without the snags and a hell of a lot fancier.

I was among world leaders, scientists and activists from across the globe. As I wandered through, I saw little houses, also known as pavilions, that countries had set up to promote their climate policies. The USA pavilion had plastered an enormous and yet horrendously sad hashtag on the side: #WEARESTILLIN. Over that week, presidential candidate Michael Bloomberg, former vice president Al Gore and actor Harrison Ford (yes, he was very cool) would all visit that pavilion, however, no official US government delegation made it to the negotiations.

The school strike movement is striving to achieve climate justice. You might be wondering what the difference is between climate justice and climate action – aren't they essentially the same thing? Well, the two aren't mutually exclusive, but fighting for climate justice recognises the injustice of climate change: those who have done the least to contribute to the problem are the first to be affected. Climate justice frames climate change as an ethical and political issue, rather than simply a scientific conundrum. We know, according to the Intergovernmental Panel on Climate Change, that gender, ethnicity, race, income and age all affect how exposed communities are to the impacts of climate change.

In order to achieve climate justice, disad-vantaged communities must be included in international negotiations, but what the United Nations climate conferences have shown over the last two and a half decades is that rich countries are reluctant to give poorer countries a seat at the table, let alone Indigenous peoples and the youth.

The schedule of a youth climate activist is a hectic one. We hop on two-hour calls and then jump onto another one, and if you're extra lucky, another one. At the same time, we'll work on assignments or send out emails or plan actions. But I've never worked as hard as I did at the COP25. Fifteen or more strikers would sit down in the morning for a meeting, discussing whose voices needed to be elevated and which countries needed to be targeted. We'd then head off to our various other meetings, rallies and press huddles, and meet up at lunch in working groups to more extensively plan our actions and long-term strategy. From there we'd race off to more meetings with UN officials, government delegations and other activists around the conference, then meet once more at 6 pm to discuss the day and Fridays for Future international concerns. The next item on the agenda would be dinner and then workshopping ideas until 11 pm or possibly even later, and then we'd hang out until we fell asleep at around 3 am. We'd be back at it at 6.30 am the next day.

One of the greatest challenges we faced was not falling into the same patterns of international conflict as our elected representatives. We needed to avoid a white-centric approach and instead help elevate the voices of those less likely to be heard at these negotiations. The opportunity for us to publicly voice our concerns and condemn inaction came in the form of a small number of press conferences. It was on these panels that young activists from around the world would tell heart-wrenching stories about climate disasters in their home countries, but what we soon found out was the media would almost solely focus on Greta Thunberg. Greta could say five words during our panel's thirty-minute timeslot and, through no fault of Greta's, the only words that would appear in the media the next day would be hers. It meant that the other voices and stories that needed to be heard were wiped from the media.

On Tuesday, the federal Minister for Energy and Environment, Angus Taylor, strolled in to the Madrid conference and spectacularly humiliated Australia. That evening I stood side by side at an event with Tuvalu's former prime minister, a man who called out Scott Morrison's climate denial antics at the Pacific Climate Summit. He was receiving an award for Tuvalu's climate action whereas I was, on the unofficial behalf of our government delegation, receiving a lump of coal. Australia had just been ranked last out of fifty-seven countries in terms of climate action.

That night I sat around with five strikers in a decrepit building that looked as if it could fall apart at any moment. The floor was slanted and the tiles were cracking all over the place. Driven by the dismal lack of action, we were planning something huge, something that could get us kicked out of the conference. We were going to occupy the stage after Greta's last speech the next morning. We knew we needed at least thirty people to avoid serious retribution, so we set upon calling strikers and securing participants.

At 3.30 am on the dot, I rolled into bed and went out like a light.

The next morning, thirty of us sat at the front of the enormous conference room. During Greta's speech we all kept glancing at each other as if to reassure each other that we could actually do this. And then the panel finished. I looked around as we all started to get up. We were hesitant until a fierce, short-haired striker by the name of Rose ducked under the barrier between the stage and us. Then we moved.

We pushed through security and clambered up onto the stage. Unsure of what to do next, we took one another's hands and sang. I turned around to see Greta behind me. I asked her if she was okay and she smiled before ducking out of the protest to avoid the media.

I can't emphasise how powerful it felt, dozens of kids from around the world who'd only known each other for a couple of days and yet here we were standing together in solidarity to demand climate justice. We were the face of change and, for the first time since September 20, I felt hopeful.

That afternoon, another peaceful protest did not go so well, largely due to heavy-handed security. By the evening, the UN had announced that all observers were no longer welcome inside the COP25 – essentially, civil society had been given the boot from international negotiations. It took hours of dialogue late into the night to get us readmitted, but we'd been warned.

The next morning, with two hours of sleep under my belt, I did a video correspondence with Channel 10's *The Project*. Much to my horror, I was awoken by a call from the producer. After frantically switching on the lights, much to the disgruntlement of those still sleeping, I opened my laptop and did the interview in my pyjamas, Waleed Aly's voice blaring in my earphones.

It was fascinating to see fossil fuel lobbyists waltz in and out of government delegation cubicles. The freedom and confidence with which they conversed with elected representatives made me deeply uncomfortable, but by then I'd learned not to be surprised by the amount of money revolving through the doors of power, not the least of which being the doors to our own parliament.

That week, the most impressive people I met were the kids who, just like me, had put school on hold to fight for a safer future. Our determination and commitment to forging a better world, however, was not shared by those actually running the negotiations. We left that conference bitterly disappointed by the world's inability to work together to tackle a crisis that already affects all of us.

I returned to Australia in despair. How was I supposed to write a book about hope if I didn't have any? As the fires increased in intensity and smoke and ash smothered Sydney, I sank further. It felt like we'd failed. But then, as the fires continued to rage up and down the coast, a nationwide sense of anger grew. People's commitment to help each other was matched by fury at the federal government's reluctance to provide adequate assistance and compensation to those affected by the fires. Not only this, but the government's blatant refusal to reconsider the lack of ambition in their beyond inadequate climate policy drove tens of thousands of Australians out onto the streets to protest.

I remember a 2018 camping trip with my family, out into northern New South Wales in the Tibooburra region. Spring is when the desert comes alive, when purple flowers and Sturt desert peas carpet the red plains, splashing colour across the horizon. As the bitumen turned to dirt, however, we realised something was wrong. Kangaroo skeletons decorated either side of the road and the horizon was bare. Not a single flower in sight. Everyday we'd be confronted with frail animals, whose exhausted bodies had collapsed besides fast-drying waterholes.

We are a country prone to fire, flood and drought, but not like this. Climate change is exacerbating the conditions that cause these disasters to become catastrophic and a source of constant torment for humans and wildlife around the world.

When you ask me about hope, I will tell you it comes from you. If there ever was a time to use your voice, now is the time. If you think your voice doesn't matter, remember that there are millions of people who feel exactly as you do and if you do not raise your voice, then who will? You could be the voice that changes everything, so please take that chance.

We need hope, but to build hope we need action. Now is not the time to place your hope in the youth – now is the time to add your voice and efforts to theirs.

We need you.

Read
'On'

Little Books,
Big Ideas

'A superbly stylish and valuable
little book on this century's great
vanishing commodity.'
Annabel Crabb

Acclaimed journalist Leigh Sales has her doubts, and
thinks you should, too. Her classic personal essay
carries a message about the value of truth, scrutiny and
accountability—a much-needed, pocket-sized antidote
to fake news.

Donald Trump, the post-truth world and the instability
of Australian politics are all examined in this fresh take
on her prescient essay on the media and political trends
that define our times.

'A delicate confession of the implications of lust and longing on a girl's sexual awakening …'
Marta Dusseldorp

On Lust and *On Longing* together for the first time.

When *On Lust* was first published it caused a media sensation: Blanche d'Alpuget wrote of a pillar of society who had molested children and of events that ended in mystery. Now she reveals all. *On Longing* caused a similar sensation, for different reasons. D'Alpuget dared to write that she loved and had inspired love in a man already adored by the public.

Here are the raw and timeless themes of the power and powerlessness inherent to lust, love, loss and death.

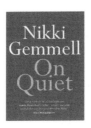

'This is the book we all need right now. Gemmell nails how to achieve serenity and calm amid all the crazy busyness of modern living.'
Lisa Wilkinson

International bestselling author Nikki Gemmell writes on the power of quiet in today's shouty world.

Quiet comes as a shock in these troubled times.

Quietism means 'devotional contemplation and abandonment of the will … a calm acceptance of things as they are'. Gemmell makes the case for why quiet is steadily gaining ground in this noisy age: Why we need it now more than ever. How to glean quiet, hold on to it, and work within it.

Katharine
Murphy
On
Disruption

The internet has shaken the foundations of life: public and
private lives are wrought by the 24-hour, seven-day-a-week
news cycle that means no one is ever off duty.

On Disruption is a report from the coalface of that change:
what has happened, will it keep happening,
and is there any way out of the chaos?

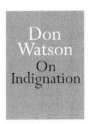

Don Watson
Watson
On
Indignation

Don Watson takes us on a journey of indignation and how
it has been expressed in his forebears. His ire towards US
politicians has a new moving target: Donald Trump.

The US President's primary pitch had less to do with
giving people money or security than it was about
vengeance. Trump exploited the anger we feel when
we are slighted or taken for granted, turning the politics
of a sophisticated democracy into something more like a
blood feud. He promised to restore their dignity, slay their
enemies, re-make the world according to old rites and
customs. He stirred their indignation into tribal rage and
rode it into the White House.

It was a scam, of course, but wherever there is indignation,
lies and stupidity abound.

hachette
AUSTRALIA

If you would like to find out more about
Hachette Australia, our authors, upcoming
events and new releases you can visit
our website or our social media channels:

hachette.com.au
HachetteAustralia
HachetteAus